A House in Memory

THE HUGH MACLENNAN POETRY SERIES

Editors: Allan Hepburn and Carolyn Smart

Titles in the series
*Waterglass* Jeffery Donaldson
*All the God-Sized Fruit* Shawna Lemay
*Chess Pieces* David Solway
*Giving My Body to Science* Rachel Rose
*The Asparagus Feast* S.P. Zitner
*The Thin Smoke of the Heart* Tim Bowling
*What Really Matters* Thomas O'Grady
*A Dream of Sulphur* Aurian Haller
*Credo* Carmine Starnino
*Her Festival Clothes* Mavis Jones
*The Afterlife of Trees* Brian Bartlett
*Before We Had Words* S.P. Zitner
*Bamboo Church* Ricardo Sternberg
*Franklin's Passage* David Solway
*The Ishtar Gate* Diana Brebner
*Hurt Thyself* Andrew Steinmetz
*The Silver Palace Restaurant* Mark Abley
*Wet Apples, White Blood* Naomi Guttman
*Palilalia* Jeffery Donaldson
*Mosaic Orpheus* Peter Dale Scott
*Cast from Bells* Suzanne Hancock
*Blindfold* John Mikhail Asfour
*Particles* Michael Penny
*A Lovely Gutting* Robin Durnford
*The Little Yellow House* Heather Simeney MacLeod
*Wavelengths of Your Song* Eleonore Schönmaier
*But for Now* Gordon Johnston
*Some Dance* Ricardo Sternberg

*Outside, Inside* Michael Penny
*The Winter Count* Dilys Leman
*Tablature* Bruce Whiteman
*Trio* Sarah Tolmie
*hook* nancy viva davis halifax
*Where We Live* John Reibetanz
*The Unlit Path Behind the House* Margo Wheaton
*Small Fires* Kelly Norah Drukker
*Knots* Edward Carson
*The Rules of the Kingdom* Julie Paul
*Dust Blown Side of the Journey* Eleonore Schönmaier
*slow war* Benjamin Hertwig
*The Art of Dying* Sarah Tolmie
*Short Histories of Light* Aidan Chafe
*On High* Neil Surkan
*Translating Air* Kath MacLean
*The Night Chorus* Harold Hoefle
*Look Here Look Away Look Again* Edward Carson
*Delivering the News* Thomas O'Grady
*Grotesque Tenderness* Daniel Cowper
*Rail* Miranda Pearson
*Ganymede's Dog* John Emil Vincent
*The Danger Model* Madelaine Caritas Longman
*A Different Wolf* Deborah-Anne Tunney
*rushes from the river disappointment* stephanie roberts
*A House in Memory: Last Poems* David Helwig

# A House in Memory

## Last Poems

DAVID HELWIG

McGill-Queen's University Press
Montreal & Kingston • London • Chicago

ISBN 978-0-2280-0125-6 (paper)
ISBN 978-0-2280-0261-1 (ePDF)
ISBN 978-0-2280-0262-8 (ePUB)

Legal deposit second quarter 2020
Bibliothèque nationale du Québec

Printed in Canada on acid-free paper that is 100% ancient forest free
(100% post-consumer recycled), processed chlorine free

We acknowledge the support of the Canada Council for the Arts.

Nous remercions le Conseil des arts du Canada de son soutien.

### Library and Archives Canada Cataloguing in Publication

Title: A house in memory: last poems / David Helwig.
  Other titles: Poems. Selections (McGill-Queen's University Press)

Names: Helwig, David, 1938–2018, author.

Series: Hugh MacLennan poetry series.

Description: Series statement: The Hugh MacLennan poetry series

Identifiers: Canadiana (print) 20200212958 | Canadiana (ebook)
  20200212990 | ISBN 9780228001256 (softcover) |
  ISBN 9780228002611 (PDF) | ISBN 9780228002628 (ePUB)

Classification: LCC PS8515.E4 A6 2020 | DDC C811/.54—dc23

This book was typeset by Marquis Interscript in 9.5/13 Sabon.

# CONTENTS

Foreword    xi

I – LATE POEMS (2015–2018)
Waiting    3
Untitled ("The bright morning")    6
Country Poems after Virgil's Georgics    7
" ... *Also in rejoicing* ..."    12
On your 18th    13
Night Words for All the Islands    14
Three Lyrics    15
Oedipus at the Crossroads    17
The Nieces    21
Rhymeless in Season    22
Quatrains    23
Quatre Études    25
Midsummer    30
High Up on the Top Floor    33
Clockwise    34
Dahlias    35
Enduring Prophecy    36
Thaw    37
Improvisations    38
Queen Anne's Lace    42
MacDonald Park: September 2015    43
Polecat Song    45
Spring    46

May Rain   47
Nausicaa Meets a Stranger   48
Alien Newcomers   50
You, as a Stranger   52
Going Away Now   54
Travel Documents for All Souls   55
*Envoi*   58
Varadero, 2017   60
Epilogues to Summer   65
Hymn for No Singing   67
O Summerland   69
Prayer   73
Approaching the Strait   74
Dinner with Random Gods   75
(*Les Préludes*, Sonnet Before Creation)   77
Migration in Orange   78
The Pantheon   79
Pacific   80
Zinnias Imposed   82
The Art History Brief Sonnet   84
(*Des tristes esprits*: Sonnet from History)   85
Farmscape   86
A Shade-Sonnet Comes   87
Imitations of Hafiz   88
November Footnote (Moon)   90

II — A SELECTION OF EARLIER POEMS
The Wrong Side of the Park   92
Old Friends   93
Getting to Missouri   95
For Bill in April   100
Vine Street   101
At the Museum   102

Untitled ("Now that my face ...")   103
Travelling   105
Summer Again   109
Rosaceae   110
Self-Portrait: as an Old House   113
Damage   115
Memorial   116
Nocturne: John Field   117
Aubade   118
Gallus Absconditus   119
Illuminations   120
Kentville, October   122
Two Views   123

last lines   124

# FOREWORD

In 1967 my father, David Helwig, published his first book of
poetry, *Figures in a Landscape*, with Oberon Press – it was
also the first book produced by that emerging small press in
Ottawa. While his fiction and nonfiction were published by
many different presses over the ensuing years, he was always,
with the exception of only two books, loyal to Oberon as
the publisher of his poetry. His last book of new poems with
Oberon, *Keeping Late Hours*, appeared in 2015, and in 2017
they published *Sudden and Absolute Stranger*, a selection of
older poems with a few new poems included, intending it to
be both Oberon's final collection of poetry, and my father's,
after fifty years of what had become an almost familial
joint enterprise.

Oberon Press did, indeed, stop publishing new poetry
books that year, but, as we might have known, nothing other
than death would prevent my father from continuing to write
poems. Although his physical health deteriorated rapidly in
his last years, and he wasn't able to follow the stringent
work schedule which had structured most of his life, he kept
writing. It was what he had trained himself to from youth,
and it was what he did, what he always did. When he was
admitted to Montague Hospital on Prince Edward Island
during his final illness, in October 2018, his partner Judy
brought a little folded booklet of his recent poetry, which
we and his friends sometimes read to him as he grew weaker.
Even in his last days, he would ask for his notebook and

scribble (mostly illegible) notes; when we came back to the house he shared with Judy in the tiny town of Eldon the morning after he died, I found a poem with recent handwritten edits lying on his desk, and on the arm of his chair a phone bill, on which he had written the first few lines of what would have become another. He could not cease to be a poet as long as he had breath in this world.

So I knew that, as his literary executor, I would have unpublished work to deal with. But I was not entirely prepared for what I found when I opened his laptop – close to 2,000 pages of material, including several completed novellas and the early drafts of several more, and also including five separate substantial files of unpublished poetry, much of it written from 2015 onwards, in addition to some individual poems, manuscripts in his office which had not been entered into his computer, and recent print-outs with handwritten emendations which were not identical to any of the computer files. I hope you may hear more about his unpublished fiction in the near future as well, but the poetry was always, in my view, the most important work he left behind.

It appears that his working system, once he moved to using a laptop, had involved keeping all of his unpublished poetry, both finished poems and rough drafts, together in large files (variously titled "New poems drafts," "Current poems," "Poems for one day publication," etc.), within which he edited different poems at different times, and from which he did not always remove poems after they were published. Some of the poems were identical in the various files, others strikingly different. Ultimately, I printed out all the files, set them side by side, identified and removed those poems which had appeared in his last two or three collections, and compared the drafts of those which were still unpublished.

Often it was easy to identify the final or preferred version; but sometimes I had multiple variant versions in front of me, with no clear way to determine which version, if any, he had considered definitive. In a few cases I had to reconstruct a complete poem from different fragmentary drafts. The final handwritten emendations of some poems did not always produce the best possible version. And sadly, a small number of poems were simply too unfinished and too fragmentary to include, despite the strength of some elements (I was particularly disappointed that I was unable to reconstruct a satisfactory complete version of a long poem about the demobilization of soldiers after World War II, on which he had obviously worked long and hard).

Additionally complicating my decisions, the largest of the computer files contained not only recent unpublished poetry, but poems which in some cases dated back at least twenty years, though others were clearly much more recent. Not all of his unpublished earlier poetry had been transferred to his computer (I found more in his paper files, including several intriguing long poems), but the fact that a number of poems had been retyped seemed to suggest that he still had some hope of publishing them. It was not my original intention to include any of these, but I found that some of them continued to stick with me after multiple readings, and I could not quite escape them. A small selection of the poems which appeared only in that file makes up the second, and shorter, section of this book.

I chose as a title for this book the first line of the poem "Waiting." This was the poem which was on his desk when he went into the hospital for the last time, and its themes and images recur throughout his final notebooks (including coloured-pencil drawings of himself as Pinocchio). This poem was, I think, his last and most serious attempt to unfold the meaning of his mortality, his aging and illness, the deaths of his friends and his own imminent death; but one which ends on a note of community and continuity, all of us joined in "the sideways book" – an image which echoes the Jewish/Christian image of the Book of Life, the sideways layout of a genealogy, and his own life's work of literary creation. The poem's first words, "A house in memory" seem to me to be, as well, a fitting tribute to that life's work, that building of a house and a universe of words, by a man who was from a family of skilled craftspeople and workers in wood, and who substantially rebuilt at least two of the physical houses he lived in over the course of his life.

The building of that house of words has ended now, and the builder's work – often, I believe, insufficiently noticed in his lifetime – will be, like all our work, subject to the long judgement of time. I am glad to be able to offer this last work towards that judgement.

Maggie Helwig

# I – LATE POEMS (2015–2018)

# WAITING

A house in memory, the long idea
perfect and simple (a door and many windows)
the right angles define survival.

A flower at heart-rise, an old man
on the bank of a deep river channel,
Mr MacFarlane's scant white whiskers:
you too will be old, rave
as the river drains the homeland,
Heart! heart! Like a father in his high old times
who hauls from the shore a broken limb.

Dark roses cascade at the brink
of falling, the whirlpool, summer's
late cluster of mossed buds. The brush
loaded with flesh-pink pigment
rises between clusters of dark time,
a garden of petals.

*Pinocchio/Revelation*

Time; does it demand analysis? If so
recall a particular moment of courage,
slow the habits, reciting baroque and multiple features
of dark minds, the philosopher on his broken throne.

Walk the aisle of silk traders, breathe rarity.
Time counts the year, the savage hope
of high recall. And lapses in barren hours
of revelation.


3

And then

in a hospital bed, bruised by some incident, accident,
waiting for news, struggling, but loyal to the decencies, truth

the end of this summer, waiting:

Choose life:

the wisdom of good will, clear words,
the hills giving up their acres of grain,
the old life, friends, some comic gossip perhaps

and Jim,

dying

4

*"on their travels"*

Too much sky, out of all measure,
in the absolute gaze of light, catch
the calculation of the mountains.
So many stars quietly going on in time,
with names as each spell comes alive.

Boat traffic, then solitude,
and the letters home. Stone
is no less remarkable at night.

After the hardest winter
never so, never so gay
as faces dwell in time
wild roses pale and dark.

We are all related in the sideways book.

The bright morning, seaweed collected
in the night at high tide, kelp and grass
interwoven on the beach. Beyond,
a drowned world, the mysterious other shapes
of sea horse, lumpsucker, sea cow
sea butterfly, lettuce, kale
which reproduce by sexual tricks,
or late and otherwise by fragmentation.
The heaps of excess gleam, ancient bronze,
shining and dark and shot with green,
muttering this is all one world,
yet the gods
tell certain of our best jokes every day.

# COUNTRY POEMS AFTER VIRGIL'S GEORGICS

*(an incidental homage)*

I

When a poet recites a fabled narrative, he finds there
his own distinctive self walking through the days,
reaching out for all the fine-wrought patterns.
A catch of sun swims through a mountainside pool.
Repeat Seneca's remark: Virgil sought ideal expression,
not truth; to please readers, not to instruct farmers.
His metric locks syllables in martial order,
like the habit of worker bees. Bless sailor's luck,
add to each moment its own divinity, apt
to the landscape, the model of sea and sky.
To grab the universe in all tranquility, set to
and modestly map out an abbreviation of being,
so bring to pass and populate a hilltop vineyard.

2

Late winter's grooved and channeled snow
thaws, air-eaten, grey-shadowed, frost
lodged deep in the soil. Spring's what's to be;
its arrival lays out the best, urgent, careful
philosophy of the Epicurean islands.
Wet snow fills the air. One last blizzard
shakes the stiff twigs. A scholar might ask
the lamed master why waterdrops, white and luminous
on the red ochre twigs striving upward,
exactly match the first silver-grey pussy willows,
catkins emerging out of their winter sleep.
Sudden in germination, such first growth
will augur in its quickness the gardener's plot –
complex, arcane, yet clear and plain as grass.
The necessary stranger builds walls of loose syllables.

3

Stone eyes lack all quickness of understanding.
Lucky the Sailor, back ashore with salt stain
on his canvas sack of gear, nominates gods
and demigods, the plump, the scrawny, swarthy, pale,
who strut among the frosted beds where bulbs
design their future under the snow in the light of ice.
Consider the wanderer Ulysses, his burnt limbs
angled over the lengths of shore, beach-combing,
canting extempore the tales of the monsters,
painting the horned skull of the triumphant.
The fabulous Aeneas will shine like tempered steel.

High noon and Simple-the-Gardener kneels on dirt,
drops seeds edged like tiny abrasive stones
into the green graveyard for metamorphosis.
Where he inters lives, the bony fingers
of this gentleman-poet learn wisdom,
and praise the labour of farming your own acres.
Laggard strong oxen plod, hoofs of the stallion
drum to the chariot's wheeled swiftness.
Lines first roughly sketched achieve a latinist
polish through habitual recitation. Aim for the life
of Lucretius, polytheist, precise in its limits.
A generation bred to the land watches,
achieves more tricks of animal husbandry: means
for raising sheep and goats, wintering flocks,
or hunting deer across the mountain tracks,
enduring plague, apprehending a cure.
The gods grow learned within their space of time.

5

Wise philosophers trace the god, the apprehensible
in each act. Which is not slave to chance
nor arbitrary event but takes its start
with fact, induction, cases held in common
named for a rule, and then exposited
by deduction as in mathematics.
To live in the upland weather is to learn
the storm signs allowing preparation
and something like a plan of safety.
Remember the misdeed of this hero or that goddess,
universal wind of the harmonic,
words to capture the nameless. The gods happen
to happen. Like metaphor. High in the stone theatre
the crowd awaits a city of words. From birth the inevitable
sustains the prayer for children of law.


6

I read hard lines, imagine for myself the wisdom
of summer events in hive and fields, the honey
that is overflow of the sun and the wise bees.
This year led to a summer like and unlike
the others. Always the nights short and adventurous,
the bright flash of moonlight over the garden.
The ruined house no longer hums with wild bees,
a groping swarm on the white pine only a memory.
The silence of wild places generates new leaves.

7

Name the poet – P. Virgilius Maro. Yes, he was famous,
just as you portrayed him in your dreams and anecdotes –
toga, well-featured face, slender upright bearing.
You might take him as the sharpest weapon of propriety,
or the approaching vivid ambition of pale Octavian,
Caesar of the mountains and countries beyond the great sea.
To work the land is to be educated in its needs;
the green of the vine wakes with the rain hours,
whose tender and expressive face calls out the ancient
wisdoms where no weak spirits brood. Speak
or keep silence as the keel runs tight
through the woven water. Everyone looks to the hills.
Strangers stand by the wild roses inventing stories
which will evoke the past, the future's mysteries,
as holy spelling teaches with all due swiftness
and the land offers bread, meat, wine.

8. (*echo and refrain*)

So bring to pass and populate a hilltop vineyard;
the necessary stranger builds walls of loose syllables.
Stone eyes lack all quickness of understanding.
The fabulous Aeneas will shine like tempered steel.
The gods grow learned within the space of time;
wise philosophers trace the god, the apprehensible.
Sustain the prayer for children of law.
I read hard lines, imagine for myself the wisdom.
The silence of wild places generates new leaves.
And the land offers bread, meat, wine.
Yes, he was famous.

Call it a banner,
the blue of noon streaming a signal
that what we have done is paid
in the wind of a just mortality.
A high wall stirs a memory of sunset.
The horizon waves blue upon blue.
Call it a banner.

Winter brings up our courage.
Named or nameless, a voice at the door,
arriving at dusk tells tales.
The woodland path is blocked
by fallen trees and the golden sun goes west,
painting the world.

The married deal out sunlight,
study the black dog
and recite the formula for gold.

Call it a ballad.
The norm of kindness breaks loose
and cries out the interlock
of blue and gold, the landscape a million
thieves at their sly corrections.
Horse, camel, donkey, the dried food
of the night desert.
Call it a ballad.

Call it a hymn.

# ON YOUR 18TH

*(for Émile)*

Now you are nearly all of what you are
(counting by eighteens) making out your way
to farness of the distance of each star
back from the final sky, tomorrow new.

And now that you are ready, heard and seen
in speech and sometime silence of the drums,
more fathers' fathers waiting to be known
and you becoming what you've always been.

The tree of always now is always you.

Lie with me under the rain, under the windows
and the lace curtains. Lie in my arms
for two hundred years of our only life. In darkness
under this rain we are everyone and his song.

Stand with me down by the shore. Everyone's
lover waits at the water's edge. Not knowing
calls back the entire truth. We are anyone now,
with the lyric hymns of the ancient goat-horn.

Lie under me, over me in the tall green grass.
The nameless nights call out in answer
to the first cricket, the speaking wind.
The green earth names us. Lie with me.

# THREE LYRICS

1

*Atom Dance*

A man so old to dream so young:
across the bedroom
trembles a wild shining.

Silver cools
infinitesimal and bright within
a minikin ion.
It whirls up the notes.

A metallic surprise:
fire's fine, finer,
the mathematics of substance
still flying:
through mystic time.

2

*In County Wicklow, 1969*

The plane comes down
out of the darkened sky
and lands in light;
morning in Ireland.

Two anglers fish on the bare
clifftops of Greystones
with tall poles, long lines
to reach under the Irish Sea.

The turf smoulders, falls slowly
in hot ash. Remembered time
will stroll the narrow
streets of the seaside village.

Morning again; a country
bus traces the hillside road,
the green way to Dublin.


3

*To Toronto*

Black tie: pale swags of pearl
hang in the night, bare
twigs lift to the half moon
far above here.
The still white mist of winter
as quiet hearts attend. A cab
surrenders the clever presence
under the hooded white uncertainty.
Song then, air of wordless lawns,
space endless.

The quiet gasp of light sufficient.

# OEDIPUS AT THE CROSSROADS

*Sing to Mr Happiness of pain,*
*naming all the husbands you once knew;*
*where you met them in the streaming rain,*
*they all must still remember meeting you.*

*Call to Mr Happiness of love,*
*back and forth the story says its words,*
*fathers, mothers, heard from high above,*
*cross the sky with other hungry birds.*

Silence is the beginning of the beginning.
Citizens gather daily at the entry
where documents nailed to the palace wall
offer the truths of antique narrative.
They will recite what is required.
Words drop the keys to the past,
and the key to the locked future.

A king stands above the law
in a mask of gold foil.
This is how the unspoken tale is said.
This is the perfect syntax of tragedy.

What will occur offers easy chances of certainty.
The future is locked in the bedroom
of the queen, the feral past.

Is the old pain serious?
All its truths are lies.

*The plague seizes children and will not, will not*
*make terms with the earth which grows hotter than hot.*

Creon, brother to the queen,
return from Delphi,
speak the god's reply.

Laius was murdered. The killer must be found,
whoever it may be. This grows imperative.

*The brother-in-law writes his name on the wall.*
*He is five minutes older and ten minutes tall.*
*His task is to lead you to where you will fall.*

*His umbrella is black and his manner is grave.*
*If you keep saving money, it's money you save.*
*Then you answer the riddle and hide in a cave.*
And now it is decreed: those murderers
at the dusty crossroad must be punished.

And the regal Cripplefoot cries, Where are they now,
in what far country? Where am I to track
the perpetrators of this bloody death?

*The old man is blind, but he stands on a chair*
*instructing a helper who isn't quite there.*
*All gods hide their secrets, though no one knows where.*

Tiresias has warned the guilty king not to annoy
blind prophets. Fate: he must be prepared
to listen to more than he cares to hear.

So it goes on. Boss Cripplefoot began
with riddles, one and then more.
The she-sphinx mumbles and gapes.

*Whatever you need, whatever seek,*
*is inexpressible, unique,*
*a traveller riding through the night*
*falls from his complicated height.*

*Darkness, suppliant, has come,*
*with the deep bell and the great drum,*
*adduces facts and will define the sum.*

The white hills offer only echoes,
of death cries, howls of generation.

What the whisper offers
to itself is the brain's darkness
where all resist and are solemn.

Each rock of these crossed roads
must be accurate enough
to offer truth, what it bodes, what it is,
the formula of tragedy,
unexpected or obvious,
the coarse telling of strangers

Who sleep at the edge of the ancient footpaths,
snorting like oily fat merchants of sour breath.
Beside the highway, bones of the dead.
I am, I plead, not of the unclean.
What the dark shadow must ever deny.

*Dream the departed, father, mother,*
*fast as wing and swift as feather,*
*cross the sky from one to other.*

*Each performer takes position,*
*spelling out regret, contrition,*
*irony its definition.*

*An oracle is a muddled thing*
*tying knots in every string.*
*Dust with gold the holy king.*

*Trapped within this sullen time,*
*hid in dismal tales of crime,*
*salvage what you can with rhyme.*

*Cry the words, then sleep, forget,*
*even though the king's beset*
*by all that hasn't happened yet.*

# THE NIECES

But what would granny say? the child voice asks,
facing a scandalous tall bedroom nude, niece
now to the strangeness of her eye. Say why
such sisters are so married to their art.

Boyfriends. The Shining Thick Moustache.
Or think of A.Y. Painter, Pal. The nieces dabble in recall,
the meaning of such memories. Selective sisters,
who bore the babies still observe

the chiaroscuro of *At the Theatre*.
The fierce, bare shoulders
recall a winter Sunday's chill,
the blent tonality.

The brass memorial plaque still shines,
on the old church wall. Oh turning glance. A presence.
Enough to be a niece, the other's daughter,
witness surviving to praise all the surprises.

down) hands delve, scrape, shape cold earth
into seedbeds oh hard fingers clutch and dig
while Piet (the Younger ) recalls
his father's scenes from the feudal life,
the labouring bodies of a common afternoon,
this day, this hour, the sheen of being,
on oil accessible to the dangers of light
as talons grub, breaking dark ground

thin breathing inspires the living seed,
quivering mystic mystery inscribes
a white kerchief on the vivid air; an apron
delineates strong haunches.

oh equinoctial muted joy, edible spring so
godly and coarse, white headkerchief
bail of eternal greenery shines
like a new god's perfection (up

## QUATRAINS

Explain the landscape? No explication, no debating
the serenity of the sea's horizon, the truancy that men
will not comprehend, the water's swift transparency. Small
as the last bits of residue, particulars of death at hand.

Our love, our need comes before and after the sighting.
What waits beyond a plain wood door when
it has not yet been opened, poets all
stricken by the harmonies of the too dangerous? And

so such beauty, such elegance waiting
in hopefulness and not to be found again
because it is and never was. In silence expect their fall,
the dead trees sustaining the hours, while you stand

among the multiplicity of moments. Unaccountable lightning
strikes far out on the stretch of ocean. Amon.
It prompts observation. Say marram grass, say red caves, say
    wall
crowned with its white death-statues. The sway of patterned
    land.

*The drift and knit of cells create the cage of bone,*
*dry sticks shaped and bleached define the white*
*forms. Over the low plain of sand rises the one*
*island, coming out of time in the only light.*

Define, my dear ones, the whole nature of beauty. Dating
from the minute of birth, the silver-pale bleach of sun
sculpts brush and bramble, the thrown ball,
and toward the horizon, the eternal slope of sand.

# QUATRE ÉTUDES

I

No ticket in your pocket,
you wait by the green fern.
Voices overhead vanish into the mist
of still winter mornings.
Broken pastry, Chinese tea,
snow on the temple steps.

*Teach me to heare Mermaides singing.*

From some yonder shore, the words
recur, the list of slights repeated.
The last wild apples must fall.

The voices, do you remember
that air of tenderness?
The steaming tea you spilled
splashed light on the waxed floor.
Grieving over lost verses,
we accommodate
ourselves to the uneasy
slowed pace of breath.

*Ride ten thousand daies and nights.*
Coal barges catch the first dawn.
A child devours the brittle pastry,
recites the unknown future.

A long throat shapes the tale.
Green silk. Who waits on the stairs?
The skin of your forearms shows white and hairless
beneath the gown. Whose fingers broke
the pastry. Who ate unspeaking.
On the low table, still, the fern, green.

Grief tunes the lost. A child waits.

The empty garden, snow
where her footprints left
a hint in the silent afternoon,
a path and how she stopped and looked
at frosted gods, plump cupids smiling
out of stone,
fat bacchus, *all strange wonders.*

Beyond the quietness
the vendor of dried herbs:
umber shades thicken on marble ruins
where a shod foot rests
on flat white stone, as the slow
photographer probes the sepia depths.

The quaint patterns
in the young man's subtle shag of beard
solicit response, warm
against the boreal wind
speaking secrets, a rod of iron
cleaving the fertile beds
of speared roots,

offers the evidence
of a human possibility,
recovered melodies, rhymed
exegesis. *A falling starre.* The garden
exhibits a vault of strange sights,
savage illumination.
A whisper renews the danger.
Someone smiling.

3

Hair bleached by the sun
of a blue-eyed country:
skies gather wheatfields of cloud
over the islands.

A hand of cards makes evening
extensive and strange, as grandparents
teach or do not teach
the wisdom of luck.
The stanza concludes with the end of dinner
under the named and nameless stars.
*Who cleft the Divels foot?*

The shapely root cries out in the night.
Deal wanton kings and queens,
hold aces close to your trembling breasts.

Take warning and retire into the hills,
one hand at solitaire.
                    *Get with child*
the cleft, your forefathers' riddle.

The white air of the northern isles
whose eyes
like blue are all transparent,
the sky as well,
the rocky hill and narrow bay,
*things invisible to see.*

4

The bones of causality grow brittle.
*Till age snow white haires*
against the confidence of commandment,
*and sweare, no where,* such presences.

You mean the voices, don't you?
Nameless now, standing in dust,
the white pulver of the marble;
such a pilgrimage toward
sculpture, what was, or what will be.

The shaped desire's consequence:
spasm, cramp, literature.
*Write your letter.* The fern teaches
its slow vanishing in whiteness.
*Who cleft the Divels foot?*
Walking, speaking in whispers,
name all that was, recall
the green fern, the splash of tea,
the dry white dust. Yes.

You must hear the voices.

Their singing.

# MIDSUMMER

I

Specific as Thursday – loose white sleeves,
blue tattoo, blonde hair pinned up,
that loose mauve batik dress – she bends to coat
the pointed pickets of a picket fence,
leaf-shaded as she paints old wood
in flat white here on a quiet street,
narrow roller, vertical sweep
up and down the narrow bands.

White with red trim, lodged in July,
her house needs such maintenance as well.

Observe her as I park the car,
while both of us give hearing to
a radio voice crossing the air.

Close by, some doctors and nurses attend.

2

Who dares sleep? Who dares sleep
in the red shadow of the tidal cave?
Deep in the nest of the high water,
who will dare close an eye?

Trees stand rooted only in air,
the forest floor waiting to fall
into the sea where broken rock
casts mortal shadows.

Where tide rises and runs, a voice calls
take me away, take me away.

3

Time needs only a thousand
generations to spell out
this its murderous grace:

osprey on pale
blue and thin cloud
high over water.

4

Song sparrow on the weathercock
wake the world at six o'clock.

Tiptop on the rooster's crest,
turn to north south east and west,
lift your beak and fill your chest,
all the air in music dressed.

Sparrow whistling out your song,
meaning neither right nor wrong,
praising neither ding nor dong,
breath magniloquently long,

chirping, whistling live toys
shape our love and thus our joys,
either, neither, girls and boys,
glad articulated noise.

Song sparrow on the weathercock,
wake the world. It's six o'clock.

## HIGH UP ON THE TOP FLOOR

A beveled mirror in a wide frame
intricate with forms, thin coat of gold leaf
swerves and curls, then glass returns
a simple rectangle, door, noon light
conveyed from mansard windows.

Beyond another door, an empty bed
recalls our brilliant white
crimes of flesh, pale marble stirred;
the brass light fixture hangs
above the stairs, awaiting footsteps.

Illuminated, your torso reveals
joint force, the polished curve
of living smooth and pale.
Manner is of time, of light, of memory.
Open each window. Await the sky.

Bland gossip speaks remembered names.
Our old pain was one way of learning.
Later, up here in the loud silence
hunger grows intimate, surviving disbelief,
declaring your whiteness and the gold baroque.

# CLOCKWISE

The vane whirls, the cock giddy
in high wind, the vertigo
of weather, where leaves
whisk their tumbling finale,

slurred steps of affliction scuff
the crazy-quilt of a path
nameless and familiar,
air tossed by the gale as

the foot-track walks
out of the cold north-east
to open later unexplained
into fallow pasturage.

A streak of dark slips through the brush;
a spirit hare haunts one edge of vision,
all accident, all lyric underfoot
the scarlet-ochre-umber patchwork.

Am an old bedazzled man on a tall stick
hurled by wind and grey ghosts,
as the needle of suchness sews up
this dizzied and tempestuous afternoon.

# DAHLIAS

Eight blooms, leaves stuffed tight
in a glass bottle on the black cast-
iron woodstove, magenta-splashed white,
gold, salvage from the last

flowery effusion of summer,
as the blade of the shovel cuts
tuberous clusters, I pull roots
from the wet brown soil of November,

and motley clustered petals flirt
at the chilled fingers' touch,
the tubers left to lie dried, inert
until as gardeners we transfer each

one to the luscious beds of spring,
defending the tender green tips
of the earliest leaves from marauding
criminal gangs of slugs,

until the tall hollow stem feeds
earwigs into the damp anatomy
of gradual, brilliant, composite
blossoms for which we two

contrive our temporary tropic beds.
Then winter comes again with all its harms,
bright November moon to shape the fields,
trees, flaunt its ring, signal of storm.

Geography abandons itself to history;
cities afloat on the fires of the infinite
falter in the elisions of our knowing.

Who will whistle the lovely notes of the bobolink,
the meadows lost? Who will warranty
the exactly certain doom of our gardens?

Beneath the wild leaves of metaphor
wind and grass and ocean shallows
seed futures which will come or not come.

Disease grows within the half-life of certainties.
We try to believe our grandchildren will forgive us
if we bless them and abandon thinking.

The inevitable rises like a great flood.

# THAW

Step by step up the curve
of the black night road,
as babble of snowmelt
rackets off downhill
to a salt inlet
lost in spruce:
the black dog stops, attentive
as a philosopher seized by wisdom.

Distant coyotes yip and clamour.

(Venus brilliant and far:
a woman prints
her solitary shadow
on a high window:
conjugates the verbs
of such desires.)

Meltwater glints, vanishes
beneath acres of snow;
months of ice loosed
in equinoctial thaw
under nameless stars.

Coyotes proclaim
recognition, blood hunger,
a season of birth.

i

*(nothing ever is)*

rare as the meaning of Monday
a handful of early gold bees crawl inside
the saffron, the empurpled, the chaliced
the simple-hearted crocus spreads
translucent petals amidst the glitter
of wild bees gathering nectar in sunlit

spring, the hurl and flash of melt babbles
urgently the fast gravity of flow unable
to overcome the helpless ineptitude
of some Ophelia's drowning, the death song, the maid
while black dog vanishes and reappears
coyote forest shining luminous dares

anyone to solve the unmeaning of free
verse when nothing is blessed today
save tumbling among petals golden
bees over etched lines of mauve when
just as rare as the daylight an ivory flower
of full moon rides the darkest day the darkest hour

one of the passing strangers says, "why you're …"
and is mistaken, call it fair, call it unfair,
I am not that one, I'm taller, right?
count it among the three-dollar nights
on the roads and trails to see and hear
in all the weathers near and otherwhere.

who else, now you think about it, (try!)
am I much unlike? doff fedora, who? why?
are you baritone high strutters, gentlemen?
or poets? I forgive you all when
lack of elegance or ditto of daring wail
from a dark witnessing corner of free fall

daisies enough for the hayfield yes
we treat the meadow like a mattress
and turn the year to burning once or twice
call out to that pretty boy, voice
deepening, at school baseball taking a bounce
in the testicles and spinning dizzy down

and almost out as the housewives golf
you watch one sophisticate herself
tennis and money dressed up for saints
and bar car charmers what counts?
the length of your kayak? so tip your hat,
trim your moustache, wink, just like that

All is evoked by the October wind
over the wide still-green autumn lawn, the tall
dead blooms of echinacea burnt deep brown,
the goldenrod at the fringes of grass,
grey fluff like a cluster of dead moths
small light collapsing into an atmosphere of storms,
the grey somnambulism of clouds shutting out
the cold distances of the sky, the far unseen,
and at the edge of a frost-touched rose garden
recurrent life invoked at the border of deprivations.
Count one small fox trotting under the long
arch of rainbow, sunlight opening on the prism
of showers, an old man of known blood
bemused, losing the names of names
as dead leaves accumulate in the brain,
the awkward sharp-thorned stems, stiff in the wind
of the dark morning, a few yellow leaves
shake, and the last impoverished buds flash
their colour, the ivory white touched with pink,
pale scarlet and the deep crimson of shed blood.

Who is it flies this bright flag of generation,
as if exempted from the cost of life,
the untroubled? Offer an unembarrassed
touch of white roses, the pink flushed
lips of an infant withdrawn to breathe or doze,
bred in a coming of age with some boy-husband,
carelessly desirable, joined for as long as it took:
another kind of belief and its object.

The clusters of birch and aspen shimmer all golden
but touched with red mist on the far hills;
at the shore of the sea where time is urgent
and crammed with gleams of danger,
the hammered silver of low-blown waves
shines over the tidal flats, the stretch
of sand and stone speaks the timeless memory of desire,
and roses, each last act of the garden,
dying, drying, death-flowers to grow again,
while an old man's poor addled brain loses
the easiest words. The roses ape his years of desire
in the absence of all that passed by,
one thing dragged us up into the past and loving,
the vivid twilight of loss and expectation,
a pallid drop of milk on a bright nipple.

# QUEEN ANNE'S LACE

*(and homage to William Carlos Williams)*

Toward departure, the lace of late summer
suspended on tall stems, giving and taking
with the day's wind, such tall strength
in a sweep of dainty parasols,
(procession of shields) as if an infinite patience
had tight-knotted the faded white points,
threads assemble a pattern of repetition,
the dim white of old pages, ivory keys.

This at the edge of the salt inlet,
and out beyond the seagrass borders,
tide's limit, where desire offers
Doctor Life his exact wisdom, all perspectives
of afternoon, the luminous emerald
sweep of shoreline grass, the blue distance.

## MACDONALD PARK: SEPTEMBER, 2015

Aged trees grow tall in their time.
Life sets out patterns serious and common,
on streets, in houses, brick and stone,
some near two centuries old.

Walking through evening into the dark
of their beauty, the passion of earth,
these hours of display prompt
hunger, delight, those memories.

Evening sky is troubled by windmills.
The young, their hungers sudden
yet purposeful, spill gasps of seed
as they swing their way through the landscape

of ghost lives. Old at the knee-joint,
limping, the later coquette flirts with recall
of the body's operatic splendours,
hope and hunger, the prim, the perilous.

Wisdom attends in its black robe
while somewhere the fatal marriages
link in words and bend awry the ceremony
the ancient books assigned.

High over the paths more loveliness,
a roof of twigs thick with green leaves.
One cursed chestnut in a small yard,
stands silent, quotidian, inevitable.

The figuration of flesh refined
into the gold-eyed artifice of thought,
the double-dancing children fill
the late white clouds with minutes of beauty.

# POLECAT SONG

Night road, tight breath, the rituals of frost,
all hackles our black dog, night-leashed adventuress
who growls deep-mouthed toward what moves
close to the earth.

At the edge of deep ditches
eyes of flat light shine, one, two, many,
whose spray, sulphurous, emetic, perdurable,
taints like ill fame, wisest of wolves letting be
what scuttles half-blind low by night grass,
engorging earthworms, grubs, the larvae
of buried wasps and more, with
the omnivore's indistinction.

Great horned owl and foolishest of dogs
(so territorial and proud),
risk the peril of assault
to be doused in vile thiols and stinking mercaptans,
learning only by misadventure like their half-wit masters,
as *mephitis mephitis*, furred and shining tail high
white on black in the chill night, feeds toward denning up
for the worst of winter, brought
to this once inaccessible island
by speculators in furs;
free enterprise biology.

We drag growl and hackles of night dog
from culvert to the wide road,
safe from the secretions
of those whose race is short-legged
into the night of the earth.

oberve it, the speed of the long fox
          stretching over a field of new grass fast
fast to her shallow-dug den, a spectre of tracks
          inscribed as the gaunt slight body passed

her clutch of this year's kits
          hidden in the rains of twilight
the youthful litter waits
          for the vixen to achieve rations,

in her small teeth, oh shiny eyes, the grip
          of canines, how loose
the body, target of leap, slash, nip.

The song's doomed grey goose
ever to be remembered.

# MAY RAIN

Thick moss covers the stumps of a rough
clearing. A spring's transparency of rain
shines on the slender twigs as foliage leafs
out and saplings spill their luminosity,
surge through slender paths of afternoon.

The newest florets unfold in the wet,
curving around like a high white collar,
reflect the radiance of arriving light,
a richly apparent range of tones surrounding
the perfect bells of the most perfect flowers.

In vivid green fields by a painted church,
the neighbourhood resigns its dead to rhymes
and rain on aged upright gravestones, each
quietly predicting a various resurrection.
The stones spell out a century of names.

A woodland road runs uphill against the showers.
Stone shoulders rise out of the sodden grass,
each pallid as a nightgown, damp puddles,
adding innumerable passages of olive-sallow
to the spring haze of every tree and bush.

The richness of creation knits a lace of twigs and buds
filtering ranges of all the forest greens
in the here and there woodlands as the thirsty dead,
multiple and rare and bright as our astonishment,
taste the sky, the fountains of life, drown.

Five thousand years. Or six. Say ten,
ten thousand years to sail the ghosts of time,
through the midmost of the earth, where gods claim every inlet
and every peak; the shore is sacred
to Zeus or Baal, to Aton or the Christ.

The pallid white men of the north, the dark
nations below the Sahara, recall the tales
and breathe them like the wind. From the heights
of an island off Marseilles or one just east of Spain
we stare over the ocean which made the world,

watch the shivering dawn wind on the shallows
as the princess and her servants walk the track
to the white sand beach beside a bullock cart
of laundry that must be scrubbed clean in the rippling
shoal and laid to dry in the blaze of sun.

But young as they are and gay and free,
the maidens abandon the cart on the track
where the lead ox stopped with a plop of dark manure.
They throw the ball and catch it with the bright laughter
of girls who have yet to learn

their ways of being women in the night.
Who run aside with catching and throwing,
and their white garments swing to reveal
the long muscles of the slender legs.
Aiee! Aiee! Aiee! Aiee! Aiee!

Roped in beach weed and crusted with salt, Aiee!
the half-drowned man staggers up, hairy and strong,
uncovered, blinded by sun Aiee! and his words
pour thick out of his throat and nose,
and the princess leans toward him, bows,

and now she leads him to the bullock cart,
offers transport – his ruined body to the court.
An outsider to be greeted: Welcome to my father's land.

(Remembered? Misremembered? That first and memorable
Greek stranger's arrival hails me back to bright lost years.)

# ALIEN NEWCOMERS

Drake he's in his hammock till the great armadas come.
*Sir Henry Newbolt*

Sunday morning, the Georgetown wharf bare, the breezes slack
under a sky of luminous overcast. Arrived in the night,
a galleon floats at its mooring by an empty warehouse. Black

lines of mussel buoys mark off the shallows. On the dock,
portable toilets, a straggle of anglers, a few parked cars,
a small crowd walks the gangplank to reach the galleon's deck.

At a folding table they sell ten-dollar tickets to view the tall
ship; on board we're offered souvenirs of the old imagined years,
and buy a DVD, a t-shirt. Silver ripples slap the hull,

the big-bellied galleon shaped like an old brown shoe
afloat, all ten sails furled and ropes laid out below the masts,
which point into the clouds above. For ten dollars we're free
    to do

just as we please, to explore from front to back, the painter,
    its oars,
to walk by an alphabet of sails to dim corners of the gun deck
where I almost see then don't the old hammocks hanged
    from the spars.

History calls out for battle, the queen is armed in steel. The trick
of war-like eloquence claims courage like a king's. Blood
flows, wood burns as cannons blast, ships drift while thick

smoke chokes the seasick admiral who flees downwind,
    pursued
by the voice of an ancient battle song, of Hawkins, Frobisher,
    and Drake,
hardy those seadogs out of Devon, their western solitude.

A sky of angled sun: the gannets dive into the sea,
All maritime contracts null, locks on the shipyard gate.
Observe the turn our steps take, how we flee

the voices of war, the ominous light of sun and moon.
Descend the stairs to the low deck where the Spanish gunners
    wait
in the stillness of the dangerous autumn Sunday afternoon.

A garden of memory, all shapeliness,
    dark tints of earth, the flare,
leaves shed, the vivid flowers survive the threat
    of killing frost,

primary colours catching midday light,
    immediate, vivid
as a boy's boast at the sight of your thick blond
    helmet of hair.

It all comes back as a garden in time,
    how it was in the chill
of that early autumn, sunflash on skin
    subtle with freckling,

the beauty of who you were, calling to what lay
    still on the simple earth,
smooth grey stone, the reflection of the cold
    at the bare riverside.

She is waiting for you, the silence said.
    The day has no limits.
The future will recall the bravest songs.
    She is still waiting.

All long ago now, your innocent womb
    knew everything, nothing.
Who could ever deny the clear blue eyes
    the sculpted features?

Memories: I talked in pig then slipped, fell
              into the river wearing
my new black hat. You found it all so funny.
              We drove back into town.

That day or soon after we found our way
              under the covers. That,
and a habit of laughter set us off
              for a winter of nights.

It seems we've survived the years of our age.
              There's more to the story,
and however many times leaves come down,
              each feels like forever.

The hardy rose persists,
each drop of blood
at the tip of a punctured finger
intent in its passing,
immortal for its season, these years
of time dying,

apart, strangely vanished,
once-familiar friends
of remembered hours,
hallucinatory fragments,
perished at the call of silence.

Peter, Paul, George, dead younger
or dead older, life resigned;
*requiescant in pace*,
we pray or fail to pray
against unpeacefulness.

All self is chosen out of our words.
News recalls time to time,
cold of breath, what pale ears hear
as tattle breeds the shapes of history,

ghost-gossip slips the eager lips ...

1

... and the child refugees plying their verbs
as if to define escape, sanctity's recall
streaming over the fallen leaves
through wind and the moonlight,
a blue background of arrivals and departures
with history's gossip shaping skies.

Oh night-child of the unleafing frost ...

The pumpkin ideogram lands on earth,
ubiquitous, a hundred candles defining,
refining *la veille de la Toussaint*.

2

White skull eating with whole teeth,
doll and gourd in the word-church.
So lovely, knife and candle
in the frame of saints. Who describes
a shadow like a star, surveys the fringe
of what could be? A parable, a precept,
a chain of syntax and at last the list of names:

the musical, the brave, the grand,
the criminal by nature, but by nature
not of the other being's other ways.

3

… in the smiles of masks, the weary day
fulfills the silence, while the infinitely small,
defended by guardians, brothers, attend
a shrine of gaiety, of expectation,
cars passing on the road like fleas
in high disguise. On the porch they strike
the wooden door.

Dusky pirate turns away, reveals
the secret of childhood obedience
and the length of her blonde hair.

In the novel, a father caresses his wife,
whose memorable *poitrine* trembles
at the advent of his strong fingers. Now
is achieved the retirement of twilight,
the eve of transformation
of the named and nameless saints.

4

The last to appear, lame and uncertain,
an adolescent sports a torn red scarf at her neck,
a mess of lip gloss squeezed in jeans,
mockery, defiance and new irony.

I did not see it on display, only
heard uneasy voicings among the leaves,
uncertainty bemused, wild for a final escape,
the lone beauty reaching for an end,
transcendence … escape.

5

Organ, the bully, the great machine
that wraps its loud heart in pious rhetoric,
waits as if all this might teach us
whatever happens that isn't death.

Time hammers on time
with a music that fells trees,
and all the lights of the city
are streaked upon the air,
using up the breath while above
the castellated towers reach far
into the darkness and with the tall
vigour of fantasy, a draughtsman
lets out waterfalls of Chinese ink
on the mandarin's mountain, two
small men and a camel slowly padding
back to the dry corner where birth
under a roof of rain begins. Deaf now
you can hear almost nothing though
the lamed and fuddled listen hard.

            The parable is learned through characters brushed
on scrolls. By morning we will comprehend
all the birds and children.
The dire night of the comic book
endures its strangeness, solitude,
leads downward through the slow descent
of the airplane into midnight, its silence,

always the invention of the hallows.

Seasons turn and return.
The night garden,
reflects a dwindling
of the dim and few hours.

The slow thought
of microphytes
floats in the brain,
a lost sunrise.

Feeding worms lose focus,
go down and down evading
the bright fields of frost
where the rare breed, vanish.

A line of whole-note rests,
designs a slow bass
of oblivion under
the skitter of blackbirds.

Where nothing dies, nothing lives.

Bleak walls of silver-tin
tremble. Far out, far off,
a lyric sky melts blind fingertips
on pewter lips and eyes,
among leaves chased in umber.

Beneath, the damp sinks
to drench the richest soil
and deep grass shines
under the haven of cloud,
the rare tones of this instant.

In the night garden, time
turns toward black
as colour reminds itself,
it is real beyond all evidence of loss.

I

*At Sea*

The space of the entire air
sweeps in; the bird bends
to windward. Seize emptiness
lest the death names overcome
where the dark ideas reside.
Speak, old skinny horse,
black and white
unite the cold currents.

Palms like giant mushrooms
shade the beach. The islands
bespeak slaughter, not moving
like the blinkless gecko.
Ashore, the cost of nakedness,
the price of golden money, the dangers
of slave hunger; the men with no language
breathe out the long dire blowgun.

Pelican among sunbathers,
all detail of beak and wing,
what will not be contained;
plump rumps in burnt repose,
a haunch of sand-walker.
This old man reclines, reserves
his white parade of all birds
long-feathered beyond
events while tall masts
seek out the joy of wind over
the sea wastes.

The overcivilized bend,
sweep the accomplishment
of young and old palm leaves.
Shorn boatminders on display,
masts in view. The firewind,
the glorious sky in love with ocean
draught between hills of sand,
the naked eye of revelation,
Innocence giving its signal, oh!
and oh!
amethyst electrics.

*Habanera*

Candlelight glows in the young eyes.
On the stone balcony, Monsignor Moot,
tall attendant, sketches grand
gestures, island nights and skies.

The bedmaid hums proletarian tunes
as words of Arabic enchant
trumpet and drum and softly haunt
palms on the shore, a bed of bones.

A delicate palomino taps
the alternate pitches of the trot,
the wagon's pace, the filly's gait
under the slender whistling whip.

Along the earthen road odd birds
take flight and vanish into night.
The narrow steel-shod wheels, though trite,
sing dim unfathomable words.

The bedmaid creates the cleanliest of floors.
A green Buick convertible crawls
back-alleys of delight. She smiles
like silk. Who's ever offered more?

Monsignor Moot drives through the park.
scent of the perfumed trees embraces,
sear and avid among the rushes,
a susurrus of wind at work.

The bedmaid puts off transparency
and smiles as schoolgirls learn to do,
imagined at sunrise, tones of blue
on a blue ocean strange as she.

*Territorio libre de anaphabetismo*

In '59 my bearded friend
counterfeit Castro comes
down from Sierra Maestra
swear by each photograph

read the letters
*guajiro*
it all depends

in '67 who soon has no hands
lingers in high Bolivia
while billboards in Russian
reject the rules of baseball

until white-skinned teachers share
green hills and the old sea
once a swamp the mute square
contains the brick cathedral

streets of chronicle
*guajiro*
streets of alphabet

those bearded wordheroes
embark with Marx
a rattling cab attends you
by the stone hotel arcade

EPILOGUES TO SUMMER

I

The loftiness of it, the lost
percentages of summer like
muscle memory in F-sharp minor.

Song whistles like a birdcall
from the sunlit porch
where the man and girl

bend shadows over the chardonnay.
A boatman steadies the canoes
in the weedy shallows of the current.

Portraits by box Brownie.
Smile, Miss Lady, smile.
The heron observes, *ah, long promise*.

Abandon the unstrung guitar;
we will perform on the Michigan upright,
ever and ever in white stockings.

2

To imagine the end, close and yet far off,
move as if backward into tomorrow
or the more dangerous illusions of today.

An idea is a blindness caught
becoming being, the tall man
isn't ever again but shadow

by the patches of black tar, blonde locks
shine with bleached summer light
while tomatoes redden daily.

The whiteness of her belly spells
the end of all amusement
and limits of silence for the lead hand.

## HYMN FOR NO SINGING

This surging instant and beyond
sheer fire, the absolute imprisoned in each cell;
green-veined saffron gapes to the pollinator
        all mouths suck, nuzzle, as unmind
           compels
        seed into furrow and down course water,
muck sluggish, soil lies drenched with fall
of rain, universe alluvial, at hand

        no metaphysic of the sperm,
only itch of summer in the grip of summer,
rose pink the membrane, crimson its shed blood,
        the goddess through her gates of storm
           come, her
        fatnesses apparent, her bright fish fed
to the bare land. Scan the glimmer
on every skin of the luminous swarm

        of atoms, boys, girls caressing
each self and other in barns, biffies, the shadow
of ruby-throated hummingbird on tall
        azured stems of delphinium, shades passing
           by meadow,
        marsh, plains of nameless grass, upland to all
lost emptinesses, and turn, oh
cellular aesthetic of excess, guessing

                    the distance of the longest road,
(petals now orange upon red, red upon blue)
          thus regeneration, soft tumults grown
                    unwieldy with joy, lilies in bindweed,
                              bitter rue
                    in the grasp of vetch, all space and air gone,
          devoured, sunk, nothing to do
but gulp, swallow, among newt, frog, toad,

                    all amphibious creatures. Wet
filaments vibrate in portraying each colour,
greedy as gardeners and bright as gold.
                    On tatterdemalion skies fat
                              miller
                    moths beat one uncertain wing past wild
cloud-busted cowgirls, the teller
of tales occupied with remembering yet

                    more blind unlikelihoods. It'll
roll on, the cycle where the cooling light grows thin,
morning dark and evening approach and touch.
                    Attendant upon planets the battle
                              goes in-
                    ward, obscured in division, a such-
ness of spiralling numbers roll and spin.
Wintering rose hips packed with seed rattle.

# O SUMMERLAND

Clouds hang suspended,
white-blonde hair shines
where tidepools gleam
on bars of sand and busy hermit crabs
prepare for war.

Time flows over the tidal flats,
mute evidence of summer afternoon,
its endless extension where the long
horizon draws its line. Concord blends
its harmonies, children a-gathering.
Step-grandfather or progenitor,
you spell out beauty, meaning, and pursue
the witness of the present-future-past.
You seek the tallest boy in every print
light-captured. Study and recall
the child's raw crayon sketch.

Long days and haunted nights,
the children falling, each one into place
like rhymes, a fugue for persons, inheritors.
Will they always match, pheno-
type in conversation with destiny,
the persona shining, brothers?

Beyond transparency,
the voice goes on, from that to this,
locked in a conversation toward conclusions
that lead us to assume too much
too soon, the boys, the men effectual,
all they were born to be,
what they have learned, to fox-trot or to waltz.
Taught to drive by my father in '54,
I learned as fast, as well
to fox-trot in the arms of the soft-as-a-kitten
sister of the town's hairdresser-to-be.
I dreamt night riders in that summer town,
four-on-the-floor in a half-ton pickup,
or nights in a black Chevy. This year
begins my grandson's driving school instruction.

Observe me, bearded man in cap and rolled up cuffs,
carrying a half-dressed boy in sodden shorts
across a pool where his calm brother stands
barefoot, fixed and curious among clams.
Tide creeps over the shoals
and at the fringe of the photograph
a proper Chinese couple, tiny child
(in a white hat, white diaper) framed by far red cliffs.
Old fat Fate winds up his pocket watch
and sleeps.
        Once, in another life, 1918,
my father, young, naive,
walked with his soldier brother
home on leave, along a home-town street
through history where the Great War led
the elder to the clouds as Air Observer
whose fall to earth and German prison camp
drove their half-mad mother to her death.
So long, so long, big brother doling out
coins for a matinee, *Beast of Berlin*,
which left my father jittery, aghast,
wrung with tears. Or so he told the tale,
a lifetime lost.
        Another son, another war,
grown plump, complacent, in my second summer
on June the ninth of 1939,
with blanket, hills of sand, my pail and shovel;
young mother smiling for the box Brownie,
as war waits us three months on.

Then sixty years, at last on a thrust of rock,
at the edge of a freshwater shore,
observe a naked boy, his tiny hand
clutched in his grandfather's fist in the island sun.
Stands taller now than his *vieux grand-père*.
His red-capped brother studies fencer's quickness,
D'Artagnan's bravery.
Lined up in jeans
and loose T-shirts we pose. Clouds cross
acres of sky. Ending a holiday,
and I am old now, bearded, half aware
that little more than nothing will endure
except what someday these grandsons recall
with every child grown into someone else.

Maintain the wisdom of such memories
if wisdom will. Listen to the duet
(quartet, octet) that vibrates in the air,
buzzing cicadas, chirp of cricket legs,
wheels whirling off to good/bad days at school,
immediate as light, mysterious as love,
bright lads grow high and handsome,
as ancients travelling on defy their fears.
They face the facts. Final desires insist.
What we intend speaks one of the kinds of truth,
and all we leave behind is history.

Imagine days of song in paradise;
a phantom ship rises in rising light.
Landmarks, seamarks, what we're given to know.
Strangers pass by the sandbanks, disappear.
Fat old Fate snores over his pocket watch,
while time spells out eternal afternoons.

## PRAYER

music recalls our questions
you once more
offering the antithetical living strawberry

the swan does not need a daily bath
to remain white
Aunt Thom journeys herself
to Bible Hill and long beyond
sweet as sunlight
or a peach on a bicycle

Thursday sloops down the slope
bright syncopations loud as metal
bright yellow toys for the not-so-old

*sanctificetur nomen tuum*

Nothing is so still
as the windless
undersea
among the scatterings
of light

while the worn eyes search
the farthest way
to the wayward
emptiness that means
all it only can mean,
in blue.

Look, the air is still here,
blue or white
as once the illusion
of all it ever is.

Who will receive this?
Far off, far off.

The black seal
vanishes a while,
bare vision defines
the space.

The sea is All. Gone. Still.

# DINNER WITH RANDOM GODS

Celebration. Not now an occasion of mere being.
Is life ever so? Open a door
and the day is fate, exception,
presence in death's arms for a rethink.

Flickering on the near horizon of far,
a signpost unbecomes itself,
revises inklings into a small man
shadows into a wiser child.

Not final the feast. Study the "as if"
as if we might yet impose meaning
on timeless hope. Downpour says
Great Charity Matches Great Hunger.

On the fifty-fourth, so many
elevators high, the storied gods speak.
The children live far away,
under conditions. The torrents *etc.*

The complex timetable of Insect Air
hovers above the streets and squares
and the dim alleys of your city,
each a possible childhood, bedarkened.

Over the lake, transcendent surfaces
of holy skies. I am the oldest man.
A room-high, room-long window
teaches invisible prayer.

The news over green soup, a hemisphere
of lightfulness, friendship, and trade.
Hours of infinity summon
possible families to rejoicing.

Lit surfaces of holy twilight
disburse waterdrops. Sun
vanishes into darkening sky.
The meanwhile is sunken islands,

and our eyes recall invisible prayers.
Study all the closed doors.
The nervous wiring articulates
the space of space, a very quiet noise.

(*LES PRÉLUDES*, SONNET BEFORE CREATION)

What comes before, a shape of abstract space
which has no presence, meaning, except the prior
of what was to be (when) and will be, the voice,
its notes prepared for a destiny of desire.

What comes before, the meaning antecedent
to the stillness of the way, soon to be
the absolute of emptiness, evasion, arrangement
selection, not to this you or that me.

This is time as king of the blankest white:
only by being a no one are we any
one at all, as an incipient night
which comes before (after) the many:

the nothing of waiting, now to know
the everything still to be, a signal at the prow.

September's plenty, afternoon's bright spread
of wings, the fullness of the yearly hatch
while wise lepidopterists study the code
and painted ladies cluster, flutter, twitch

the frilled edge of a wing, the awful eyes
staring from the pale underwing, the gaze
of mystery, predation, orange and black lace,
scarlet amidst elaboration's maze.

What ever might be as brilliant, as intense,
as absolute as breath, see it begin
cross multiples of hatchlings on the pink

blossoms of stonecrop sedum, succulents,
*Vanessa virginiensus* coming in,
unfolding, fluttering. Now attend. Watch. Think.

# THE PANTHEON

Their mysterious living in the images
of all the other worlds, cliffs, west and east
over-watching the grey sea, the atheist
north Atlantic beating on the embodied air.

Hail the daft old foreign gentleman
limping along the green rows. How to honour
his wound, the loose-woven trousers sacred
to memory, the titanic baptism.

White with sun, oh grace of wisdom,
wisdom of grace, three matched girls, headless
deities, a naked homage fore and aft.
Hail the wall, space for all the divine ones,

tall verticals before and after time.
Realizations come dressed in clear air,
bare-assed scarred captains, grizzled beyond
dignity of expressive speech, the boys of war,

unemployed philosophers define the names,
eternal and figurable in stone. Marble fathoms
the lies and the cries of murderous self-love,
shaped in dancing, illuminated by the oculus.

The secret of the dome, how made in what hands,
is unknown to even the slickest architects
from Adam to Brunelleschi, yet all (ALL)
seek altars for the innumerable.

*(reading Ross Macdonald)*

The shade of solitude seeks words
in all of the grand-shadowed houses.
Big Sur, like a woman averse, hides
in this the country. You will never find it,

arriving where it begins and ends
at the door to a mansion twice passed by,
where the slow-spoken
private eye has not yet put down a foot.

We contemplate the west horizon,
the long downslope of the highway;
wild orange poppies, and beyond the cliff,
the unchangeable mortal tide

of the ocean kingdom, its narrow way.
The bridge clings to the steep mountain,
high and so slender crossing
breathless the river valley.

The vast, slow unrelenting surf
unreels from the bright shores of Japan.
At the rough campsite the greedy blue
Steller's jay proclaims one desire.

The sun, dangerous and not eternal,
yearns all the while through the long noon,
expectant, staring beyond the ripples of the sea,
riding the rare light of comprehension.

The author learned his trade on Bloor Street.
The sea is unknown, be wary of rockfall,
wait on the very highest bridge, drink
only wine like ice that shatters in the mouth.

With virtuoso insistence you must splash
petal by petal, brushstroke by brushstroke
among the plants, as emblematic whim
flames the leafage of the autumn plot,
preparing branches, those on which will flare
circles of crimson red and darkest pink.

Visionary fire, and so high comical,
so dutifully shining its new shoes,
dogmatic toes waltzing remember hours,
counting the strokes of perfected creation,
the intricacy of manufacture
touched by violet in the twilight shadows;
late flowers spill from chemistry and wit.

Every event, every bright-eyed flower, demands
three lines of explanation with clean words
as stem with selected leaves, a flower intense
as acrobats who spin the pigment, blood
of the Saturday night circus, or a bright
mauve curl of decor shapely as whittled tack.

Berries of rowan carved out of the sun,
unique this seasonable afternoon.
The drumming hoofs, the quickness of the wagons
lit by crazed eyes, svelte dancers stride ashore
where wheels of ancient cycles spell with zeds.

The lively colt flares up, gallops toward
the farthest windy corner of rising land.
The dog will join October's escapade.
At every crossroad, signs spell light and dark,
reveal an emblematic jug of flowers,
the holiest lover (once!) a plump *artiste*.

Among the yarrow, tall dandelions, goldenrod
thrive in old August, enriching with gamboge
the close ground of the dark
acres, the sweep of maturing soy

in the shadow of a holiday.
Weeds! she cries out, *les mauvaises herbes*!
They play at infinite division.
They carry at their sides warm hands.

I would lie down in a ditch to feel
the richness of this mellow Asiatic tint.

## (*DES TRISTES ESPRITS*:
## SONNET FROM HISTORY)

Toronto, 1910, at Christie Pits,
a bake-shop perfumes with yeast the streets nearby.
Westward on Bloor – immigrants from Leeds,
at work now, *'e's the chap's gone mad for pie.*

*Luvely*, the lad said, *ay, better than 'ome.*
Shadows from there recount hard times in Leeds.
Yorkshire Club on Saturday night's become
his seat for cribbage, a ready deck of cards.

Pegs count fifteen-two, a place to start,
where lads may all pitch in, share the delight,
*tha mun bring tart for all,* some young lips cry.

Nightshades of laughter float close by,
and he devoured on the darkening street
the cardboard plate along with the cherry tart.

the ditch, the sog
of autumn rain,
as two black heifers

mud to the knees
cross the log and wire.

Cloud over the bay,
running east-west
past luminous
shores of grass.

Long point
where the seals
gawp and grunt.

In the ditch
the workman's knife
sheers thick reeds.

A red and white dory
rests in a pasture.

# A SHADE-SONNET COMES

Events fragment succession, and then
failing to make the present persist,
observation falls aside, and so
once more defines change as cost.

Now all sings morning, the beach predictable,
time's result of the rainfall, pebbled
evidence of minutes gathered, slight
as the digits of the lucky child

who came from the blankets very early,
on the air the throat-catch of wood-smoke
and the visiting boy grasps the tiny car
in his hand, the rhythm of wavelet lurks

innocent as breathing, the fast ducks beating
their shade of travel against the light. And then?

I

All the animals are listening to your sighs
beyond a veil of green leaves.

And they sing. The messengers forbid
spiked shards and knives.

Don't try, you cannot analyze the taste
of love, you cannot measure darkness.

Whose white little hands will quench
all the years of your sadness?

The wise will teach you how to remember
the games you knew in childhood.

"So easy," Hafiz tells you. Bring
your heart to learn laughter.

"So easy." Set free your wishes,
all the hankerings of your imprisoned soul.

2

Yes, OK, I know, I go on repeating myself,
but brainless and heartsick, I have no choice.

A grey parrot facing a silver mirror
gets his instructions: "Say this."

Red rose and black thorn both have erupted
from the dark of the garden's rich soil.

The shattered edge of a broken heart
offers the gemstone's absolute gleam.

So I'm a lush, drowning in wine;
it's better than the rattle in an empty jug.

All lovers everywhere howl and whoop
singing the hymn tune of the Great Desire.

Ask me, say: "Hafiz, why are you always
besotted in some tavern doorway?"

*Standing here I can follow forever*
*the road that comes and the road that goes.*

## NOVEMBER FOOTNOTE (MOON)

and nightly trace our steps up slope and down
the wanton skunks and foxes watching
out of the ditches, woodlands, light
catching their bright eyes

how gentle for October
the drift toward November
and the moon full or set to be

how gentle
yes

and the clouds illuminated
yes

and the dog leaps in darkness
oh yes

the harsh voice of the wind, morning
watching the silver moon setting
behind the bare trees as, yes, sunrise comes on

II – A SELECTION
OF EARLIER POEMS

*(for Tom)*

In your lost poem lie
elms by the courthouse cut
in an epoch of disease.
(The trees attend in their silence
the flight of a hurtful lover.)

A new elm risen in your name
stands three men high tonight
on the wrong side of the park.
(You camped eastward, on West,
now in the obverse of living.)

In your crazed clairvoyant city
fearless children climb, who
explore a geography seen
from the back of the map.
(You are nowhere and with us.)

# OLD FRIENDS

No plot to all the memories,
only the intervals and episodes
of our two voices talking.
Thirty years. Things as they are.

Friendship is a kind of silence too.
A landscape most remarkable for being known.

Restless, irritable souls,
but once at a restaurant
you sat indoors waiting for me
while I sat outdoors waiting for you
for most of a long hour.

"Is he romantic?" your daughter said one night
and "No," you said, which wasn't quite the point.
Somehow we chose to skip the poetry.
Prose has its passion and a longer breath.
We watched each other live our other lives.

In the last years, a continent apart,
and I kept moving further off.
Notes, arrangements, phone calls in the night,
breakfast in Montreal one good summer day.
You were studying god and struggling to breathe.
I was counting your cigarettes.

I missed my last chance to visit and the news
that you were dying couldn't find its way.
Another kind of silence. Things as they are.
Now if I sit waiting, no matter how long,
I think you won't arrive.

It is too much to know, my dear.
It is too soon.

# GETTING TO MISSOURI

i

> *Plaisir d'amour*
> *ne dure qu'un moment.*
> *Chagrin d'amour*
> *dure toute la vie.*

Just south of Cleveland
a boulevard called Chagrin

Along the bed
in the interstate motel
a horizontal mirror
set to catch
the fugitive act of love.

North, south, the moment
of spring advances
and retires, a dance
in season.
      As once
years past, the roads
unrolled the world
just at spring.

Leaving, your sleepy voice:
a last goodbye.

I wheel the Pontiac
over the hills of Kentucky.

There are too few words
for green, for all this sun-
smitten green.
         Dark cedars
stand sentinel against
the brilliant slopes.

New leaves. Still water
caught in traps of earth.

Old sewn bonnets: women
bent in these fields.
         You,
old one on your porch swing,
tell me your story!
         Crow,
hawk, buzzard, what is
that soaring black bird?

Would I choose to forget you
if I could?

iii

Travel, like every ecstasy,
is discontinuous. Mile by mile
events break free
from their attachments, eyes
burned awake by new landscapes

as when eye and hand break free
and millimetre by millimetre
celebrate your graces

which are in whose keeping
tonight?


iv

Roadkill: blood and mess,
raccoons, opossum, skunks,
a single coyote.

And the slender-legged deer.

I see them in the night,
dainty and wide-eyed
in the killing lights, fine
bodies slaughtered
by machines.

One of us (who?) stands
helpless, imperilled
as the fast wheels
bear down.

v

This is south.

At the ceiling, the fan
spins with a sound
of tiny distant tin birds.

Grey morning rain light,
strange voices; trees
spread green hands
in the sky.

Old rain words come to mind.


vi

Once moving, never stop.

It is noon in the city:
men and women kneel
in the old cathedral
by the great brown river.

Mansions boarded up,
streets deserted, all
fallen into disuse.
Black faces wait.

Guilty dreams, a ruined
house, bodies
of murdered women
in the wreckage.

(Once this ended
with a lie.
Can loneliness, grief,
ever tell the truth?)

The body is the first dream, and music
is the second, while the landscape
of love waits like the far darkness
of the spring night.

Health and song and rare words,
the power of thought, all these, old friend,
the luck of the draw. Choices
fall into our lap like a basket of stars.

And God deliver us from goodness:
save us for the commonplace quotidian,
the falling body, this dream
that allows us to share laughter.

# VINE STREET

Thinking, until you could not feel the cold,
looked in and out of other doors and windows
until you could not see the snow or falling
or know where you would come.

To the height of the small houses built to the measure of the
    poor
(old childhood nonsense songs, oh remember
the lanes, relieve-oh, and the rat champion)
to the length of short streets
with short names, one frugal syllable,
not the space for much in those blunt views
to the low roof of a low house, winter and the mail,
porches, sheds, icicles, curtains, a wooden fence.

Passing by at the end of the block, you see it,
small and still and wrapped in a red blanket,
anonymous at midmorning carried down the steps
to the ambulance for delivery to a place of the dead.
It is male or female, packaged for transport,
found silent in a room with a calendar and dentures
and is taken away.

Catching sight, turning, you are on your way
down the short street and another and into the city,
dying alone today, feeling the cold, and later, as in another
    country,
in the red blanket of blood, snow passing a window
down the roads through the empty woods, you are back there
with the dead but also with the others, thinking.

Here where all time is timeless
bronze, wood, shards, broken stones
mounted and set in place,
my grandaughter's small voice,
heard where we name the nameless,
lays benediction on the bones,
the valleys where the dinosaurs rejoice,

on stolen tomb and altarpiece,
grave clay of antic armies
risen from ancient night,
mysterious and right.
So wonderful the shining glass,
all wonderful, she cries
in her annunciation of delight.

Eternity grows Blakean,
the metamorphic child
is blonde and bright and ours
for breaking open doors;
although the future's shaky in
our age of growing old,
its falling's falling outward among stars.

Now that my face is channeled,
like a relief map of river country,
I must have come to know time,
but imagination fails
at the long arithmetic,
a million volcanic years,
mass extinction of species
during thousands of millenia.

Too long. Dried bones
on the museum floor never
lived, and Pharoah
stepped out for a breath of air
just yesterday.

Start by saying
this is a wet February night,
my lover warm by my side,
and I have dreamed
for twenty-two thousand days.

Or make each second
a century, each midnight
eight million years.
Nothing works. The Palaeozoic exists
only in the heart of the wise machines
that read the pulse of breaking elements.

Try to imagine fire
at the earth's core,
light years of sidereal time.
Imagine it's time for bed.

Clouds covered today's eclipse.
My lover sleeps warm at my side.
Try to imagine the last
long division.
                    Or zero.

# TRAVELLING

1

An upper berth: I'm going
feet first into the future,
snow between the cars.

Morning in l'Estrie,
incursions of light,
the slow arrival of colour,
the secrecy of house, barn, schoolbus,
pale blue shadows.

2

The trained observer sees
the beautiful fields
of winter, black verticals
on the white snow,
gold-silver shining
of water against a sky
as dark as plums,
honey-pale grasses,
umber weeds, the flat
frozen marshes, grey thickets.

The will is ordained
to assemble fact into
a semblance of meaning.

Beside me the slack sullen
beauty of a stranger's face,
sleeping.
        Outside, the dark
red clumps of dogwood.

3

A mystery bought for a dollar,
one scant achievement of order, then
the blonde cashier off work
smokes her cigarette in the occasional rain.

Translations to and from poetry.
The lost tropic caught
the candymaker's son.
Hart Crane goes into the sea.

4

Small self after small self.
The parade thickens.
We are singular beings.

The question of cold –
the eye of time,
modern apparatus, or just
the ice of genius.

One day passes in silence.
Oh words, I knew you once.

5

Effect of mist rising:
the little islands clear
and golden against a distance
of white fog,
here in the mysterious
space between stars.

6

The almost empty streets
of Sunday morning.

The city reminds you of everything.

Mouth, eyes, and silly
soft laughter as the young lovers
wait for the bus, beautiful,
fresh from the night
and arrant in a sweetness
common as time.

The cells in the spring garden
of their bodies dying,
being born, dying, being born.

No one can give them ever
a morning as tall and perfect
as this Sunday in Toronto.

Everything makes them smile.

## SUMMER AGAIN

The world being what it is, evident and so quick,
so lovely, what is a man to do? Bumblebees
breach the pollened deeps of the lush
peonies, nuzzle, tumble, roar in the fat
flesh of this voluptuousness blossoming. Roses
open their tight buds, scarlet, crimson, pink,
petal by humid petal. By tall mallow the low
banks of pansies pigment the hectic light.

Decorous, we avert our eyes from the pale
and so-new bodies of the adolescents
in their fluster of sensual innocence
at play, green upon green upon green in triumph
on every side, and now even the ancient rain
comes down upon us gently as careful hands.

# ROSACEAE

I

Half price survivors
tempt the greedy eye.

Gravedigger's work in small:
the iron hoe now pick and mattock
tearing sod, breaking hard
red earth, mining stones.

The sour sore ineffectual spine
aches, bending, pivoting,
as the mattock swings,
gores roots and stems, hauled free,
space broken, manured
for the horticultured roots.

Tight buds spread to the chosen
display of tones, coral, lemon,
rag rainbow rare as all crimsons,
this botanist's wonder – subzero,
snow and harsh wind holding it harmless.

The story is always old and always new.

2

On the table
the cultured rose
sheds petal, petal,
each little scarlet
blood-drop
an old word
on old wood.

3

At the window you
stare as the overcast
opens to brighter
illumination. A vision
shapes itself, the tall man
offering to come to you
out of the sky, womb
of the white rose of light.

4

tall, prolific
wild in the wild garden
secrets
   of inwardness
so long
confounded
    in this ancient rose

in the wild garden
cells
   conjoin five pink
tongues
    hungry  metaphors
        appearing
        vanishing

5

      The cold rooms
abandoned by the world:
      a house is a machine
for loving, she said,
      and falling, a blossom
beyond its age, sunlight, moonlight.

      The sentimental observer
          hears
    from an empty bedroom
a ghost voice thinly incanting
      Moore's "Last Rose."

# SELF-PORTRAIT: AS AN OLD HOUSE

Made wise by solitude, desire, the found
and placed grows resonant. Trees
shade the sunlight to a delicate green.
In the storybook quiet, a distance of bright water
beyond the open doors, traces of women

(long years ago now) and summer glows
on the skin of a second-hand saint.
Birds of morning, of evening, sing.
Yes, perfection requires absence. No one home.
Late sun flickers its pattern on the walls.

In possession of only this: the very beautiful
in the frame that makes it so, as from the blue room
a naked man stares at brilliant reflective water.
In a treetop quietness, salvage: tools, a forgotten
queen, a gymnast in silhouette, hair, bones,

all curios selected for their perfect shape,
rarities taken among the abandoned,
an eye creating inexplicable riches.
Behind the placed, the recreated, dim
histories you may neither own nor deny.

Metaphor will not explain itself, only that alone
and obsessed, whim is the highest knowledge.
You are the summary of so many days,
nights, splendour, joy, right and wrong
courage, the explorations of darkness, dawn.

Each chosen colour is perfect, yellow for morning,
green for evening, blue for the oncoming night.
(He grows anonymous in the long darkness.
Lightning's jitterbug and the stars surround him
and in secret he has worked out his ways.)

# DAMAGE

A man attends at the edge of a great lake,
as the shimmer and dazzle and glitter
come and go on the mirrored surface.
The pale shapes, the dark, silhouettes
sustain this weight of light. A landscape
frames the astonishing bay, calm precincts

where a young mother in her white skin
grows plump and marked with breeding.
Celibate boys hack at the standing timber,
while somewhere a clear-headed biochemist
invents new disasters in his perfect room.
Bodies unmarred by personality gaze

at each other though the blinding summer glare.
The children fall into brightness
as other children once fell, crying out.
We see there is no joy without damage,
nor damage without such glittering joy.
The old lioness studies it with cool awareness.

# MEMORIAL

Afternoon vanishes into the sky with
hapless, well-meaning dialogue.
We sit together in the recognition of loss.

Beyond stone walls, mullioned windows, the cold
light of spring: she who has proved mortality
attends this public event as a bravery recalled.

The personal, impersonal occasion of praise
sends me beyond the dutiful listening
toward a long-past conversation, how she found
means to speak the name of a secret lover.

Later I came to understand what I hadn't known,
recall it now in the quiet of this public act:
how it became possible, the child, the garden,
freedom to speak his name at all hours.

# NOCTURNE: JOHN FIELD

A whisper, and a night bird cries
as listeners hear the song again,
men loving women, women, men.
The candlelit performer tries
to say desire tells no lies.
A glint of distant stars, the ten
fingers articulate, and splen-
dour breathes and fades, the whisper dies.

Remembered notes recur all night
as strangers in the dark and cold
take hands and join like word and rhyme
like song and echo taking flight
from dusky earth where young and old
float in the quietudes of time.

Now the insomniac greets the hint
of day, eventual relief
from nightlong lingering, a stint
in hell, an endlessness of grief.

The lovers waken as the earth
turns to the light, and each one sees
a bare specific thing's rebirth
as flesh that's apt for ecstasies.

Whether the tint of rising day
is flags and trumpets or the flow
of pallid, pearly, silvered grey,
sky and ground dimly a-glow,

inevitable night is gone
with this inevitable dawn.

## GALLUS ABSCONDITUS

Domestic fowl in exile,
a rooster on the lam flees
under the apple trees
hides out behind a pile
of deadfall, all the while
pecking bugs and seeds,
nourishing rooster needs,
complacency and guile.

*Gallus gallus sub malu*,
jailbreaker on the loose,
outsprinting all who follow,
retires beneath a spruce.

(Says Wisdom, even clever cocks
will not forever balk the fox.)

# ILLUMINATIONS

i

Walking the dog at night, moon shadows cast
on the field – silhouettes of bare branches, trunk –
by a star lost to sight, long since sunk
and now reflected to this hard crust
of refrozen snow, pallid and blue and laced
with black, a mechanic miracle, a link
to all that may be done with shining, wink
of shutter caught on silver or replaced
with digital memoranda, how the light
entering a tiny metal case encodes
face, landscape, a luminous presence,
agitated electrons, all the bright
dots assembled, particles at nodes
of flow, a simulacrum of existence.

ii

The item has been marred by cliché, space junk,
tired rhymes, and yet is overhead,
a white circle of light, and so instead
of the old word call it that. The drunk
sang incoherences to the light-circle. We thank
the radiant geometrical form for madness, tide,
and maybe weather. Seedlings should be set outside
only after June's full coronal is in the bank.

As I drive home fullness hangs over me,
light in the lightless, this its grandest phase,
yellow in rising, white among cloud-flowers,
regular, predictable, yet rarity
enough, however depleted by our ways.

The empty room's blue glimmer in the small hours.

I am abroad in a forest of the first age,
a lucky survival, history's accident
(like a translation from a truant page
of time), its filtered illumination pent
within a valley where tall rock walls shut off
the barbered, the designed, the utilized.
These stately trees have endured centuries, safe
somehow from harvest or from fire. Amazed
I walk among the immense hemlocks, pines,
look upward into the clustered, needled crest
of foliage. Spacious archaic paths, greens
of fern and moss, and everywhere a blest
ceremonious quiet reigns,
joy's afterward, suffering's, music at rest.

A vantage point, the muddle seen from above
in diagram: the declaration of truth will hold
for all known cases, so we are bold
to claim. A curve is the long locus of
a point obeying a set of rules. The shove
and muscling of particles as the dice are rolled
infinite times in an instant – the untold
vagaries graphed. This is what we approve.

Or not. Perhaps I have said all this before;
the mind fights the same battles with the mind
all its days. As my eye comes very near
all's clutter, blurred, shapeless, growing more
and more blotted, outsized, and we find
it queer, and lonely, being here, being here.

(last lines, discovered on a phone bill)


*the language of the waterway*

*the name*

*the train's route through bliss*


*to*